Talking to S

Behind the Scenes With a Radiologist

By

Carolyn Jourdan

The names of the doctors in this book have been changed, as well as certain other identifying features, to protect the privacy of both physician and patient.

ISBN 13 E-Book 978-0-9972012-2-2

Table of Contents

Prologue

This small book is a companion to ***Radiologists at Work: Saving Lives with the Lights Off***. It is a narrative that chronicles my experience of shadowing a radiologist while he worked.

We developed a singular relationship over a period of fifteen years while sitting alone together, in the dark, in the bowels of a large teaching hospital, in the wee hours of the morning, meeting only once every few years.

Our intermittent association ended up giving me far more insight into radiology and radiologists than I ever could have imagined.

Here is the story of what happened on those seven nights.

**Even the darkness is not dark to you;
the night is bright as the day, for darkness is as light with
you.
Psalm 139:12**

MEETING JAY

If we weren't actually beneath the surface of the earth, we might as well have been. There was no natural light anywhere. There were no windows in any of the gadget-packed rooms that lined both sides of the corridor. The Radiology Department was like a high tech animal burrow.

I was led down one nondescript beige hall after another until my guide stopped in front of an unmarked door. This one had a keypad on the wall next to it. My escort punched in a code, shoved the door open, and gestured that I should go in.

The room was dark. I took a hesitant step across the threshold and stopped. The heavy door gave me a nudge when it closed behind me, but the place was so dimly lit I was afraid to move. I needed to stay where I was and wait for my eyes to adjust to the gloom.

I could hear a man a few yards away talking rapidly in a language I didn't recognize. I looked toward the sound and saw a guy in a white lab coat sitting on the other side of the room with his back to me. He was facing two images of skeletons mounted side-by-side on a lightbox.

Ah. That must be the radiologist.

I could barely make out the features of the room, but one thing was clear—I was surrounded by skeletons. They were everywhere. Black and white images of bones, bones, and more bones seemed to cover every surface. And if that wasn't enough, there was a life-size three-dimensional model skeleton dangling from a stainless steel pole against the far wall.

At least I hoped it was a model. From where I stood it looked like it might be real. I felt like I'd walked into the scene near the end of *Romeo and Juliet* where she wakes up in the

Capulet's tomb and says, *I do remember well where I should be.*
And there I am.

The doctor's stream of high-speed chatter never slowed. It
was an eerie tableau. A man was sitting alone in the dark, talking
to skeletons.

I wondered if they ever answered him.

I stood still, listening, trying to sort out what the
radiologist was saying. I assumed he was dictating findings on
the x-rays he was studying, but his speech was so rapid it was
impossible to follow. I felt sorry for the transcriptionist. I hoped
she had a way to slow down the playback so she could listen to it
at a manageable speed.

As I waited, I entertained myself by recalling every
synonym for darkness I could think of. By the time I got to
stygian and *crepuscular* I'd worked up the courage to shuffle up
behind the doctor. He didn't stop talking, but he turned his head
slightly and I saw he was holding a handset or microphone in one
hand.

I continued to watch and listen, hypnotized by the obscure
patter. I became so lulled by the darkness and the
incomprehensible blabbering I was startled when he abruptly fell
silent.

When the room was quiet it felt even more like being
inside a mausoleum. The doctor set the handset down, quickly
removed the films he'd been looking at, and replaced them with
new images. Then he picked up the handset and resumed
dictating.

The pictures were like nothing I'd ever seen before. They
were peppered with of all sorts of metal bits like wires and
staples, artificial joints, pins, rods, jewelry, and birdshot. I could
recognize some of the shrapnel, like the wire that held a sternum
back together after a chest operation. But most of it was a jumble
of unidentifiable debris that seemed to be floating out in space.

My father was a family doctor who had practiced solo for
forty years in a rural area of East Tennessee. I'd grown up in and
around his office and had watched him read countless x-rays of
his own patients. I'd seen only one that looked anywhere near this

busy and it was the product of a snafu where the nurse-technician forgot to ask a female patient to remove any superfluous items.

The resulting picture was of a skull wearing metal cat-eye glasses, a full set of upper and lower false teeth, dangle earrings, and a necklace. The images I was seeing now weren't nearly as macabre, but they contained an extraordinary amount of junk.

As time went on I gleaned that the radiologist either didn't realize I was the person who'd driven more than 200 miles to meet with him, or he didn't care, so the next time there was a hiatus in his high-speed soliloquy, I spoke.

"What's all this hardware in these people's guts?" I asked.

"What hardware?" he said, still not looking at me, but turning his face slightly to one side.

I stepped forward and pointed at two metal bits in a man's pelvis.

"Vasectomy."

Then I pointed at a piece of metal in a girl's abdomen.

"Belly piercing." Then, as he finished reloading the lightboxes, he added, "You'd be amazed at what people are piercing these days."

He picked up the handset, but before he could start yakking again, I asked, "How do you sort it all out?"

He faced the fresh skeletons and began to rattle off a monolog that was so smooth, at first I thought he'd resumed dictating, but he hadn't, he was answering my question.

"You encounter different kinds of visual clutter on x-rays," he said. "The first are technical artifacts, things that aren't really there, flashes of light that are just bogies being caused by the technology itself.

"Then there's metal hardware such as screws and plates and rods placed by orthopedic surgeons to stabilize fractures; surgical clips and staples from gallbladder or other bowel surgery, wires used to close a chest after heart surgery, pacemaker wires attached to the heart, shunt tubes inserted to relieve fluid pressure buildup in the brain or spine. These things will all show up on x-rays.

"Metal shrapnel and bullets, or swallowed metallic foreign bodies also show up. As well as retained glass fragments or road debris from where a patient burst through a windshield and bounced along the interstate.

"Wooden splinters usually can't be seen. They're almost indistinguishable from the body's soft tissues because they don't contain metal.

"Superimposed on these internal objects are items that are outside the body like EKG leads, I.V. lines, buttons or snaps on clothing, hooks and wires in bras, jewelry or piercings, eyeglasses, anything in the patients' pockets, and glass eyes or dentures."

He paused for a moment, a Professor of Radiology, waiting for any follow up questions.

"You don't always talk about those things."

"I do if it seems relevant. I usually describe the position of all the inserted lines and tubes, and I list the surgical staples and wires since they're clues indicating organs that may have been altered or removed. The rest of it is usually irrelevant.

"I hardly even see the bobby pins and monitor leads and other artifacts anymore. I simply subtract them with my eyes."

"How?" I asked.

"We encounter so many visual distractions in x-rays, we have to learn to disregard them. After a while it becomes an automatic reflex to mentally subtract cluttering objects from the image."

I stood there, dumbfounded. I couldn't imagine how he did it.

"It leads to the occasional bizarre result," he added.

"Like what?"

"One of the best radiologists I've ever known once read a chest x-ray without mentioning that a screwdriver was driven into the center of the patient's chest.

I flinched at the unexpectedly gruesome picture painted by his words.

"A student," he said, "or a beginning resident would've noticed the screwdriver and commented on it, but the more practiced eye unconsciously dismissed it as an extraneous object overlying, or underlying, the person.

I snorted.

4

"I'd laugh, too," he said, "except I did the same thing once with a golf club. When I saw it in the x-ray, I unconsciously assumed it was outside the body. I must've thought it was lying beneath or atop the patient, when actually the head of the club was up the man's rectum."

The mind boggled, but I knew radiologists saw a lot of unusual things jammed into a lot of different orifices.

"You have to understand," he said, "we rarely see the actual patient. We don't get to see what the clinician is seeing. We don't have the full, real-world context."

Wow, I thought. No *real world context*. What an understatement. It was a euphemism that nailed one of the many distinctive aspects of radiology.

Not being physically present with the patient made it much easier in some cases, but it was a horrible handicap in others.

I form light and create darkness, I make well-being and create calamity, I am the Lord, who does all these things. Isaiah 45:7

THE DARK LORD

One Month Later

The room was a kaleidoscope of disembodied parts—fingers, legs, spines, skulls—a tableau of stark images in pearl and gray, backlit by a pure white light.

The utter colorlessness was like a landscape seen in the prolonged twilight of a Scandinavian winter. You suspected there were lots of colors out there somewhere in the world, but there simply wasn't enough light to discern any of them.

Even Jay himself was a study in visual restraint. On the rare occasions when he tore his gaze away from the walls of bone and glanced at me, the eyes that glinted over the top of his wire-rimmed reading glasses were silvery gray.

This time I was watching him work in a tiny radiology reading room somewhere near the emergency room. It was an amazing art gallery where every variation in density was nuanced in a range of grays that seemed to be infinite.

The only light was horizontal and blasting straight at him from the viewing boxes on the wall. It was surprisingly flattering, even filtered through films depicting the horrors of the last couple of hours in the ER.

During this second session of watching him work, the word bone-ologist popped into my mind. What an unusual environment this place was—the boneheaded world. It was a dark world, the underworld. And Jay was the lord of it.

After that first meeting I'd been hooked, entranced by the strange romance of a reading room and I'd asked Jay if he'd let me visit again. He'd graciously agreed, so now we were together in a small space where I had to stay sharp and watch my toes or they'd get rolled over as he zoomed back and forth in an office chair in front of the biggest lightbox I'd ever seen.

After my father had been in practice for several years he'd upgraded his single viewer to a double one with space to hold two x-rays side-by-side so he could compare an earlier film with a later one. That had always seemed luxurious, even flashy, to my family. But Jay's lightbox was industrial size.

In this cubbyhole he could study about ten square feet of x-rays at a pass—six films across and two down. That was twelve images at a time if the lightbox was loaded with plain films.

But if it was loaded with CTs, there were twenty smaller images on each piece of film, so twelve of those meant he might have as many as 240 images available at a glance.

It didn't matter how many he loaded, though, because there were hundreds more, even thousands, where those came from. He'd been at work since 12:30 in the afternoon the day before. I'd joined him shortly after 1:30 in the morning, so he was now thirteen hours into his shift.

I sat behind him in the dark and gazed at the pictures while he dictated into a telephone recording system. Again, I felt sorry for the lady who'd have to transcribe the long hours of his breakneck techno-babble. But any troubles Jay, the transcriptionist, or I had paled in comparison to what was spewing out of the ER.

He put his handset down and began sorting through a stack of large brown envelopes on the counter in front of him. Each of the paper sleeves contained one or more x-rays. "Are you bored yet?" he asked, as he rummaged through the pile.

"No," I said. "How could I be? It's all so beautiful."

At this he made more than his usual half-turn to display a cheek. This time he turned three-fourths of the way around so I could see his expression of disbelief.

"Honest," I said. "It's a privilege to get to see the...." I stuttered for a moment, embarrassed to say what I was really thinking, then decided to come out with it, "... the image and likeness of God."

Jay made a scoffing noise, and said, "More like the image and likeness of hell."

Then he turned back to his work. He pulled half a dozen old x-rays out of the jumble of folders to compare with the new images on the wall.

"Maybe you and me looking at this is like what God sees when He looks down at us," I said. "Maybe the earth is the Lord's emergency room."

That got a laugh. I hardly knew Jay but I suspected it was a rare thing for him to laugh while he was working.

He asked one of his nearly invisible helpers to retrieve previous films for another of the patients whose x-rays were hanging on the wall so he could tell if things were different, and, if so, whether they'd changed for the better or worse.

He was constantly being assisted by silent technicians who had a genius for remaining close by, but just out of sight, like subterranean butlers in nether-nether-land.

With deft movements honed by years of practice he swiftly removed the films he'd already dictated his findings on, and flicked new ones onto the wall beneath metal retaining clips and tightly stretched clear wires that looked like fishing line.

"You have strange ideas," he mumbled.

Despite his austere veneer, I could tell he loved his profession. He seemed to thrive in a job where he worked mostly alone. And even then he preferred the night shift where humans were even more scarce. In deference to his solitary nature, I tried to stay outside his range of vision and be as quiet as possible. It was easy to dissolve into the pictures and float along on the sounds of the medical jargon.

Jay was an anatomical genius. He had to be. It was wonderful to watch. He could discern the fine points of the internal structure of a human body no matter which way it was turned. He'd learned to alter his own perspective to match that of the various imaging devices so he could always navigate comfortably. And he'd seen so much he bore a library of pictures within himself to guide him as to what was normal and what was not.

Before I'd sat with him, I'd thought normal was a lot more constrained than it really was. It didn't take long to learn that *normal* covered a mind-boggling range of possibilities. Reading radiographs wasn't like using a road map where you could rely on precise drawings.

Even so-called normal people, were often wildly asymmetrical. To Jay, if something wouldn't cause a problem, it was normal, or at least normal enough. X-rays were like road maps created with the idea that as long as you arrived at your destination in one piece, you were good to go.

I saw images where people's bladders looked square. That bothered me a lot, but it didn't worry Jay. There was a film where an elderly woman's osteoporosis was so severe you could barely make out her ribs. I wanted to cry, knowing her bones could be broken by the least thing, like a sneeze or rolling over in bed.

A man had a bullet in his brain. The hollow point slug shattered on impact and made a starburst pattern that was narrow at the entry point in the back of his skull, then widened, and dispersed into a spangle of fragments as the projectile flung itself toward the front of his head.

"How can he still be alive?" I asked.

Jay's eyes flicked over toward me, then back to the image. "He's probably been declared brain dead," he said, "but it would appear that his body is still being carefully tended for organ harvest."

"Oh."

I watched Jay look for the cause of mysterious pains, at fractures and stones and cancer, at a thirty-five-year-old woman who'd been beaten, a seventy-year-old woman who'd been hit by a car, and at a man whose artificial knee was hurting.

There was also a forty-year-old woman *in extremis* whom we'd revisit more than once an hour relying on a variety of imaging devices to try to get a diagnosis. She had so many blood clots, they'd installed a filter to try to keep them from getting to her lungs and killing her with a pulmonary embolism, but it looked like she might die anyway.

After several hours I noticed something so unusual I forgot myself and blurted out, "Wow, finally someone who's not fat!"

"Cancer'll do that for you," Jay said, reaching out to touch several pale gray blobs in the woman's lungs.

"Oh, sorry," I mumbled, mortified.

I rolled even farther back into the dark after my *faux pas* and sat silently while he dictated another ten-minute's worth of impenetrable medical terminology to his invisible coworker on the other end of the phone line.

Growing up I'd seen a vast range of medical problems. I had a biomedical engineering degree. I thought I knew a good bit of medical jargon, but I was wrong.

I would experience this over and over with every radiologist I spoke to and not only with medical terminology. Without exception, I found radiologists to display vast, elegant, and eloquent vocabularies. They frequently used English words I'd rarely, if ever, heard spoken aloud. Or they used familiar words in a context I'd never encountered before.

They said words like *instill* when they were talking about using gravity to load someone's colon with a barium enema, or *lucent* to describe a spot on a radiograph that was darker than the surrounding area because the x-rays had penetrated it more easily, or *morselize* to describe cutting a body part to bits.

Jay's description of what he was looking at was as far from a normal person's as Shakespeare was from drunken karaoke or your neighbor's vacation photos were from National Geographic.

I began to see that in this particular specialty the doctors had to develop a superb vocabulary because their dictated monolog might be all the communication they would ever have with the attending physician. They were under a lot of pressure to perfect each digital message before they corked the bottle and cast it out into the electronic sea.

I couldn't get over how much pure junk was strewn across the people who were getting x-rayed. I couldn't understand why at least some of it wasn't being removed or swept to one side before the technicians took the pictures. I brought it up again during a lull in the action.

"These people look like they've come directly from Mardi Gras to the x-ray room," I said. "How do you decide what to look at?"

"You're touching on one of my worst fears with this," Jay said. "I often don't know *why* I'm being asked to read a particular x-ray, especially in the ER reading room. The clinical information hasn't had time to get to me before I have the image in hand and they're in a hurry to have me read it out, so I frequently have to read blind.

"I have to look for *anything* that might be wrong. If it's an abdominal image, for example, I have to try to figure out if the person is having pain from being constipated, or has just been in a car wreck and might have trauma from a contusion, or a ruptured spleen, or a broken back."

"I never thought of constipation as an issue for the ER," I said.

"It's one of the most common things we see. People have a bellyache. It could be caused by any number of things, but often it's constipation. We'll look at the film and dictate our findings and their doctor will break it to them as diplomatically as possible that what they really need is a trip to the bathroom."

"Are you saying you might be reading an abdominal CT or an x-ray and not know whether the person is sick or injured?" I asked, astonished.

"Yes."

"What clues do you look for?"

"Everything—free fluid like blood, bile, or urine outside the confines of its normal location. A fracture, a torn liver or spleen, enlarged lymph nodes, distended bowels, stones, kidney obstructions, aortic aneurysms...."

He stopped speaking and turned back toward the wall of horrors.

"Is that all?"

"No."

"That's pretty scary."

"Tell me about it. We've had to do it that way for years, but the computers they're going to install will finally fix it, we hope. Until then I will continue to have nightmares that some night a mentally ill person, or a drunk, or someone on drugs will be brought in having just swallowed a box of paper clips and I'll ignore the foreign bodies and dictate about lung lesions!"

Jay stepped on a floor pedal to activate a motor that refreshed the images displayed on the huge lightbox. The rows of lighted squares ran on a conveyor system built into the wall. The twelve films he'd just *read out*, dictated notes on, were slowly being replaced by twelve more.

Wow, I didn't know a lightbox would do that.

It was cool and at the same time horrible. It was like we were playing *Wheel of Misfortune*. Jay was doing Vanna's job.

When I asked him how the monstrosity worked, he said there was a tech on the other side of the wall who removed the films he'd just read and loaded new ones.

Of course there was. The unseen person who manned the backside of the giant lightbox and who unloaded and reloaded it whenever it moved was yet another member of the invisible legion of co-workers who were relegated to non-speaking roles. The situation brought to mind Egyptian slaves who spent their entire lives fanning a Pharaoh or untouchables who waved fly swatters over a Viceroy of India.

As the night progressed I kept track of the rotation of the lightbox. There were fifty rows on it, forty-nine that held images and one left open so they could change the light bulbs. When I commented on the number of images and the massive size of the rig Jay said, "This is only one of the auxiliary reading rooms. There are others."

"Where?" I asked.

"We have rooms that serve the Surgical, Cardiac, Medical, and Neonatal ICUs. And viewing stations in the suites for ultrasound, whole body and neuro-CT, MRI, fluoroscopy, and nuclear medicine.

So far I'd seen only this small room off the ER and the huge Central Reading Room deep in the bowels of the Radiology Department. I'd had no idea that the radiology department had tentacles that snaked throughout the sprawling medical complex.

The next time Jay stepped on the floor pedal and the conveyer rotated to mechanically refresh the pictures, I realized it bore an unnerving resemblance to a point-blank view of a tank tread. And it sounded like a tank clattering toward you, as well.

I tried to understand what it meant that for half his life, Jay had sat impassively in front of such a behemoth, like a Buddhist monk. He was part of a unique order of eremites who sat alone in the dark, having walled themselves up and taken a vow of silence toward the outside world, but who dictated with desperate rapidity to people who weren't actually present, mimicking prayer without ceasing.

12

We all sacrificed ourselves at work in different ways, but I knew I wouldn't have lasted very long in this place. I'd have been roaming the halls looking for patients who were still awake for someone to talk to.

During the years Jay had been a radiologist, he'd deciphered an inconceivable number of pictures, tens of thousands of CTs, MRI's, nuclear bone scans, angiograms, colorful lung scans, smudged black and white gallbladder studies that looked like dirty fingerprints, mammograms, fluouroscopic images, and the so-called *plain films* which were the things I'd always called *x-rays*.

Then there were the utterly baffling images produced by ultrasounds, or sonograms—the interpretations of which, as far as I could tell, were akin to reading tealeaves.

A career in radiology was like a thirty-year-long slideshow or an endless PowerPoint presentation. How could anyone focus, or even stay awake, for that long when they were alone in a dark room?

I certainly couldn't. When I regained consciousness from either nodding off or zoning out, Jay was speaking into his handset, "A sixty-eight-year-old female who fell off of a swing...."

Falling out of a swing was a silly sounding problem but it had resulted in several broken bones. I wanted to ask why a woman who was that old would be swinging hard enough to fall, but I didn't, because I was afraid the answer might be that she was senile, or drunk, or that the swing was a cover story for domestic violence.

I preferred to imagine a perfectly healthy, happy, and sober elderly woman enjoying a swing that hung from a spreading maple tree in her front yard. I had to invent happy scenarios for a lot of things I saw that night.

As the evening wore on, it became obvious that an endless variety of unpleasant situations would continue forever—world without end, amen—sickness, injury, broken arms, kidney stones, dislocated shoulders, cancer.

It was heartbreaking. And mind-numbing. And soul-destroying.

A forty-year-old man was near death in the ER from an unknown cause. The ER doctor wanted to scan the patient to see if he could find the problem. And he wanted to use radio-opaque dye, but that carried its own set of dangers, so he came to talk to Jay about what to do.

"If he's already in kidney failure, you're gonna have to dialyze him anyway, so go ahead and use it," Jay said. "You'll get more information with the dye."

A few minutes later a pulmonary specialist appeared in the doorway. He asked Jay a bunch of questions about a patient. They went on and on, way too long. It gradually dawned on me that this doctor had not yet laid eyes on his patient. He'd neither examined him nor spoken to him.

When he left I mumbled, "God help us all."

"What?" Jay asked, without turning around.

"A doctor is trying to treat a human being who is suffocating to death by extensively questioning another doctor who has also never been in the room with the patient."

"There's a reasonable explanation for that."

"Really?" I said. "I'd love to hear it."

"The patient is in the ER, so the pulmonologist knows he's being well looked after by an ER doctor and a nurse. He also knows we have images available. He swings by here on his way to see the patient because he knows we can show him things he would never be able to see in a physical exam.

"By coming here first he might be able to make a diagnosis immediately without having to waste time examining the patient for anything and everything that could possibly be causing a problem.

"One way or another, whether by making a diagnosis or by ruling out a lot of potential problems, the images will give him a lot of information. Coming here first saves time and helps the patient."

Okay, I believed him, but I still didn't like it. I silently prayed for the patient. I hoped someone was with him, holding his hand as he gasped for air.

Jay was dictating his findings about a kidney cyst when yet another shadow loomed in the doorway. I didn't know who the person was, but something about this guy's harried stance indicated he might be an ER doctor.

He stood quietly and listened to Jay dictate for a few moments, then shouted, "I don't give a shit about his kidneys! The guy *hung* himself! I need to know what's going on with his *neck*!"

Jay glanced over at the doctor with no expression, then turned back to face the wall of images and immediately switched to talking about the man's cervical spine.

So this was what happened when emergencies got ahead of the paperwork. And this was what it meant for the radiologists downstream.

Now I understood what Jay meant by *reading blind*.

**For you are all children of light, children of the day.
We are not of the night or of the darkness.
1 Thessalonians 5:5**

IT'S NOT ALL BLACK AND WHITE

One year later

I was back in the black and white world.

This time I was aware of the pressure Jay was under when he was at work, but for me *The Rad Cave* was still a novel diversion from a world awash in sunlight, particularly since I bore no responsibility for anything that went on there.

I watched him read images for an hour or so, then when things got quiet, I held my arm out, and said, "My forearm has been hurting."

He didn't touch me or ask any questions, he simply glanced over for a nanosecond, and said with his thousand-yards-from-the-bedside manner, "Probably a...." He said some word I didn't understand that ended in *-oma*.

I didn't know much, but I knew that some kinds of *-omas* were cancer. I didn't like his diagnosis and resolved to never ask him another personal medical question.

It was understandable that, as a radiologist who worked at a big city hospital, rather than as a family doctor in Strawberry Plains like my father, Jay might develop a tendency to suggest potentially fatal diagnoses.

It would be easier allow your worst-case-scenario tendencies to run rampant if money was no object and if you weren't the one who was going to have to break the news to an actual patient face-to-face.

I didn't say anything out loud, but I couldn't stop myself from mentally comparing Jay's practice with my father's. My father knew his patients, as well as multiple generations of their families and countless cousins extending laterally to the horizon, so he tended to diagnose things that could be cured by taking an aspirin or by lying on the couch and watching a couple of episodes of *Hawaii Five-O*.

16

My father was actually in the same room as his patients. He saw them in color. He talked to them. He touched them.

My father told me many times that he'd learned the importance of being a source of comfort and reassurance, and of always giving the patient hope. He believed it was his job to always give hope—never to lie or mislead, but to muster calm, warm, genuine positivity in every case.

Jay held out one of his own arms and said he'd been having some pain in a forearm, too, and realized he probably had something incomprehensible, but which also ended with -*oma*.

"Do you think *everything's* an –*oma*?" I asked. "I've never known anyone with forearm cancer in my life and yet here, according to you, we've got two cases in the same room on the same day. What're the odds of that?"

He frowned, but I continued, "You should think about switching over to –*itises.* That's what Daddy gives everybody," I said. "The only thing that's wrong with us is that I've been typing too much and you've been flipping too many x-rays onto and off of the lightboxes. We've got some kinda *muscle-itis.*"

I could tell I'd annoyed him.

"If you saw what I saw," he said in a bitter tone, suddenly vehement, "you'd be thinking -*oma*, too. Everybody in this place is dying and a huge percentage of them are younger than me!"

He looked away, and then mumbled, "The whole world is dying."

I was shocked. He must've had a rough night, or a rough day that had bled into a rough night.

He glanced down at his beeper, then stood up suddenly, sending his rolling chair flying backwards. "I've gotta go up to a Surgical ICU to confirm that a tube's positioned correctly."

I followed him though a winding maze that spiraled up several flights of stairs, half running to keep up with him. It had been years since I'd run through the halls of a hospital at night, but I'd done it countless times as a child.

If the next day wasn't a school day, my father would take me with him when he was called out in the middle of the night. I'd sneak along behind the nuns who glided down the halls in their long black habits, white wimples, and veils. I'd be as quiet as I could, and they'd always pretend not to notice me.

Here, at this time of night, there was no one to hide from, so I let my footfalls echo up and down the empty hallways.

We went though a type of double-door I'd never seen before. One side opened in one direction and the other side opened the opposite way—at the same time. It looked like a Rube Goldberg device to enable you to burst through a doorway unexpectedly and knock two people down instead of one.

At the end of every hall, in the corner, a blue light was mounted vertically at a height that ran from my knees to my shoulders. They looked like bug zappers. I pointed at one and, breathless from the long sprint, said, "What're these for?"

"It's a UV light to kill germs," Jay said.

"Wait a second," I said. I went close to the device and spun in a slow circle, taking a shower in the blue light.

"That feels better," I said. "Don't you wanna do it, too?"

He shook his head and smiled slightly. Apparently he was forgiving me for the *–oma* criticism.

The Surgical ICU reading room was extremely sobering—even more than the one off the ER. I wouldn't have thought it was possible, but it was. I'd seen a lot of x-rays in my life. Hundreds of them. But I'd never seen anything like these.

These patients were in dire condition. Not a single one of them had been able to hold their head up enough to keep it out of the frame. I could see their faces in the chest x-rays. All the heads were slumped forward, chins resting on chests. It was unbearably moving.

I stared at the ghostly grey lips that were never smiling. Some of the people had their mouths open. I couldn't tell if it was because they were unconscious and their jaws had gone slack, or if they were gasping for air. They might've been in pain, moaning. Each of the images had to be read through a pattern of swirling EKG leads, plastic tubes or braces, and whatnot.

We looked at the x-ray of the tube that Jay had been called up to check and he explained that when someone was on a ventilator, you wanted to be sure the oxygen hose went well down inside the chest, that it hadn't gone down into the esophagus by mistake, and that it had stopped before the airways branched off heading toward one lung or the other.

"You want both lungs to be able to get air," he said. "If the tube gets shoved too far down, perhaps due to the patient thrashing around, it will go into the right or left lung and that prevents the oxygen from reaching the other lung. People on a ventilator aren't able to take care of themselves, or speak, and often they aren't even conscious. If they have a damaged lung and oxygen is being sent only to the bad side, it could be fatal."

When he was finished I followed him back to the the little reading room off the ER.

I was becoming fond of the small room. It was like a chamber on a submarine—dark, cramped, and crammed with complicated hardware.

This time it was nearly wall-to-wall with people, either sprawling in rolling chairs or standing against the walls. Half a dozen radiology residents had come by to do the same thing I was doing—to watch and ask questions.

"Professor," I murmured to Jay.

"Can't help it," he shrugged. "They need an old guy to answer questions, and although it pains me to admit it, that would be me." He touched the wisps of gray at his temple and gave a wry smile.

The residents were a funny lot. Exhausted. Devoted. Full of questions covering everything from who had tickets to Allison Krauss to *Where's the pancreas?*

They showed Jay the films they'd read out for the ER physicians during his brief absence. One of the x-rays was a side view of a spine. Jay leaned in close and counted the vertebrae out loud, rapping each one with a red wax pencil as he went down. "L-1, 2, 3, 4…. See? The transverse process is broken off.

"It gets snapped off in severe impacts. Always look for that. It's a trivial injury by itself, but it's telling you the person went through a heck of an impact, so you'll need to look for other injuries, like to their kidneys."

He circled each of the snapped off bits of bone with the wax pencil and then immediately wiped the marks off with his thumb so as not to humiliate the young doctor who'd failed to see the fractures.

A resident immediately grabbed the phone and called someone to let them know about the error.

Jay reviewed the films they asked him to, saying things like, "This is a normal…." "No, that won't cause any trouble…." "Well, yeah, but that isn't what they need us to tell them about right now."

They sorted through stack after stack of old films, comparing them with the new ones, looking for changes that might have occurred over the last three years, or last three days, or if the person was really sick—over the last three hours.

Seeing such a rapid succession of images scared me. Needing to x-ray someone every few minutes to see what was happening couldn't be a good sign. But things could get even worse. And they did.

I looked up and a handsome late-thirty-something man was standing in the doorway with his gloved hands held up in front of him like a scene from a medical television show.

"Can you take a quick look for me?" he asked. "We just got a patient off the helicopter and they lost his pulse in the hall. I was hoping you could take a look before I open him."

Jay rocketed to his feet, slipped past the surgeon in the doorway, and flew down the hall in the smoothest, most graceful sequence of movements imaginable. It all happened extremely fast. He was running but making it look like he was only walking, like a shoreline bird outrunning an unexpectedly big wave.

He went into a glass-walled room adjacent to a CT scanner. When the surgeon and I got there, a young man was lying very still on the table, disappearing slowly into the maw of the machine. So far he'd made it from his head down to the middle of his chest.

We stood behind the technician, watching a computer monitor that was displaying the results of the scan. Jay leaned over the technician's shoulder and studied the image as it emerged.

There was a brief time lag between where the scanner was working and the images that formed on the monitor. When the lines started painting the abdomen, there was a lot of white. Just underneath the skin of the man's belly was a patch of pure white that didn't fit in with the greys on the rest of the picture.

Oh, I knew what I was seeing. Jay had showed me a big white area on a radiograph before. He'd said it indicated an area of massive blood flow. It was an aorta. I looked again and thought to myself, *This guy had two aortas.*

I wondered how a person could have two aortas, then I heard Jay say, "He's torn his spleen."

Jay pointed, and told the trauma surgeon, "He's pouring contrast medium from a splenic artery into the abdominal cavity, but the bleeding is being slowed by the pressure in his belly. This looks like more than two units spilled so far."

Oh, not two aortas, the man was bleeding to death. Or, since he had no pulse, by standards anywhere except here, he was already dead. But because he was in a Level 1 trauma hospital and had everyone's undivided attention, maybe he wasn't *totally* dead—yet.

I hoped that was the case. They had a lot of fancy equipment and many smart, daring people in the building. Maybe they could resurrect him.

"Looks like a seat belt injury?" Jay said, shooting the surgeon a questioning look.

The surgeon nodded, still holding his gloved hands away from his body. He said, "A bit of chest discoloration, but no visible injury otherwise. When I open him, he's going to want to exsanguinate. Okay. Thanks. That's just what I needed to know."

The surgeon left the scanner area and Jay headed back toward the ER reading room. I took a last glance toward the patient. His legs were disappearing into the machine.

I caught up with Jay, wondering when they'd stop the scan and snatch the dying boy off the table and whoosh him to the OR, but I didn't ask because I could tell he was unsettled.

Jay saw me looking at him and snapped, "Why do you come here?"

"I like it," I said.

"You're insane," he said, and quickened his pace, leaving me behind.

I trailed him back to the ER reading room. The residents were gone now and he was sitting in front of the lightboxes, staring at his night gallery. I sat almost directly behind him as far back as I possibly could in the tight space, so as not to annoy him any further.

He just sat there without picking up his handset to dictate. I waited, forcing myself to remain quiet as long as I could stand it.

Finally, I said, "I've spent most of my life hanging out with doctors. My Daddy worked incredible hours, day and night, seven days a week, year round. If I wanted to spend any time with him, I had to follow him around while he was working. Following you reminds me of times spent with him."

Jay didn't turn around, but he stood up again and made a diffident gesture indicating I could follow him some more if I wanted to. He race-walked the length of several hallways and then jogged down a couple of short flights of stairs. As usual I had no idea where we were going, although I did notice that we were losing altitude.

He stopped in front of an unmarked door and punched some numbers on a keypad. The lock clicked open. He went in and I followed close on his heels not knowing what to expect. Automatic fluorescent lights flickered on and cast an ugly green glow onto the room.

It was a small cafeteria and we had the whole place to ourselves. I surmised it was for doctors based on the fact that just inside the door was a table with several open boxes of doughnuts. Each box was a sampler displaying a variety of types: chocolate-covered, crème-filled, sugar-coated, rainbow-sprinkled, and more.

The back wall was covered with open shelves loaded with all kinds of potato chips. Another wall was lined with refrigerated cases displaying squashed white bread sandwiches asphyxiating in plastic, pieces of mummified cherry pie, and small bowls of garishly colored Jell-O with mysterious and horrible looking foreign bodies embedded in it.

I stared at the mangled sandwiches and said a word Jay had taught me, "Triturated!" He gave me one of his professor-nods to confirm that I'd used the term correctly. It meant ground up or pulverized.

The room was crammed with poisonous junk food, arrayed in lavish, nearly pornographic, displays and hidden away behind a locked door so stressed-out doctors could binge-eat in secret.

22

Jay grabbed a banana.

"You're kidding, right?" I said.

I went for a thirty-two ounce plastic cup and spewed crushed ice and Diet Coke into it while he poured himself some coffee. Next I scored a bag of Cheetos.

When Jay saw what I had, he put the banana back, then reached out with a big paw and grabbed three individual-serving boxes of a multi-colored, sugary-looking cereal. He set his coffee on a nearby table and tossed two of the boxes of cereal next to it.

Then he ripped the top off the cereal box he was holding, tilted his head back, and poured the contents down his throat—dry—while standing up. He chased the cereal with black coffee.

Then he sat down at the table and stared at a blank wall. Apparently this was how a radiologist relaxed.

I was afraid to sit with him until I knew which way things were headed, so I strolled around the room exploring the trashy treasures. The food was apparently free. There was no cash register anywhere and no place to leave money.

It was strange sort of paradise—an altar to the devil in the basement of a temple dedicated to healing. Doctors keyed in a password and offered up their own health as a sacrifice to demons in exchange for healing their patients.

As I walked around I ate a few Cheetos and took a huge drag of Diet Coke. I could feel the salt and carbonation and caffeine instantly take the edge off. Okay, so the devils were keeping their half of the bargain.

Then, to kill more time I decided to fix myself some Raisin Bran. But, unlike Jay, I got a Styrofoam bowl, a carton of milk, and a plastic spoon.

I turned back toward his table. He sat bolt upright, rigid, still staring at the blank wall, holding his remaining two boxes of cereal—one in each hand. I wondered if he'd simply bite through the side of the box on his second carton of Super Sugar Bits or whatever it was called. No telling what he'd do with the third box, maybe eat the whole thing, cardboard and all.

It took me two trips, but I carried all my selections over to his table and sat across from him. I kept my eyes on my food while I ate, to give him privacy, and to avoid the buzzkill he was emanating.

Eventually he spoke. "This is not what I bargained for when I went into radiology," he said. "It used to be the quietest, most laid-back part of the hospital. The atmosphere was almost *contemplative*. Now we have surgeons waiting on us to read for them while the patient bleeds out.

"We get all the DOA's now! Why are they bringing them to *me*?"

I felt sorry for the guy. In the last two decades radiology had utterly transformed. And the pace of change was increasing. His job had morphed into something unrecognizable.

"It's th holocaust that never ends," he said. "It goes on and on forever. Even when I go home, I don't sleep. I just lay there replaying all this pain and suffering and death. I don't have a life. I'd like to have a life someday."

I nodded in commiseration. He had a hard job. I decided not to mention the people who laid asphalt in full sun, or stooped for endless hours picking fruit, or needed a hose to breathe like underwater welders. Instead, I tried to refocus the conversation.

"Seeing your work has certainly given me an appreciation for dense medical jargon," I said. "I used to think it was pompous to use words that regular people couldn't understand, but now I see the benefits. You're being as accurate and concise as possible, but you're also speaking in a language that's so obscure you can talk right in front of people without giving anything away.

"Like when the surgeon said the guy was gonna wanna *exsanguinate*. What a word! You wouldn't wanna say *bleed to death*."

"Yeah, specialized vocabulary helps. Not enough, but some."

He was stilling looking at the wall. The one without anything on it.

"There's something *bad* wrong with these people," he said. He tore his eyes away from the blank wall and looked over at me, "It's so wrong they *all* have to be in the hospital!"

I hadn't really thought of it that way, but of course it was true. "I guess I'm lucky I'm too stupid to perceive most of what's going on here," I said. "And I'm just hanging out every now and then. I don't have to stay on continuous high alert for years so I can save everybody."

He had the saddest expression. I was sorry I didn't know him well enough to ask if something else was wrong, besides the obvious.

"If I ever get to thinking I've got problems," I said, "sitting with you for a few hours, or even a few minutes, shows me how wrong I am. I freely admit I couldn't do this every day like you do. I respect and admire you for your dedication. The patients would thank you for it, too, if they could."

If they even knew you existed, I thought, but I kept that last bit to myself.

We finished our junk food in silence. Lunch, in the middle of the night, in a bolthole underneath a hellhole.

Jay never did get a bowl, or spoon, or milk, but he recovered enough to eat his other two boxes of cereal through the perforated opening at the top, a handful at a time. When he was done we left the little cafeteria.

As soon as the security door snapped shut behind us I had a nearly overwhelming impulse to ask Jay to put the code in again so I could open it and see if the lights had gone out when we left, like a kid playing with a refrigerator.

We went back to the ER reading room without encountering another soul. I was sitting behind Jay when a gurney bearing a profusely bleeding person was rolled past the open door.

"At least you won't have to get any of *that* on you," I said, hoping to cheer him up.

"Oh, it gets on me," he said, still bitter. "You can't slough it off. At the end of the day this stuff sticks. How could it not?"

I should've kept my mouth shut. He hadn't recovered his equanimity yet. I didn't say anything else, just swiveled back and forth in my chair nervously.

"In my training I rarely saw acute trauma cases," he said. "The hospital where I did my residency was specialized. It didn't deal with typical emergencies like car wrecks.

"Now I get the worst stuff first! This is not what I signed on for. I can't stand it. I hate it. I hate my life."

I thought he might be upset about the young man who'd been bleeding to death. "When will you find out what happened to him?"

"Who?"

"The guy who was bleeding."

"Never."

"What do you mean?" I said, unable to comprehend not knowing how a patient fared after treatment.

Jay extracted a pen and a creased scrap of paper from a pocket and scribbled against his thigh, asking, "He was Zinc Zinc, wasn't he?"

"What?" I said.

"The patient with the torn spleen. In those kinds of emergencies we use code letters to identify them until we can get their real names."

"Oh," I said, shocked.

"It's just temporary. They cut people's clothes off," Jay snapped. "When a guy's bleeding out, they don't want to waste time trying to get his social security number and his insurance card."

"Okay. But are you saying you've gone all the way from Alpha Alpha to Zinc Zinc? How long did that take? I had no idea there were so many unconscious people lying around—or flying around. Is there a war going on somewhere?"

"That's what this place is like!"

"I'm starting to get it," I said.

"I try not to lose track of people," he said. "I *care*."

He reached into the pockets of his white coat and his pants and even his shirt, pulling out half a dozen bits of crumpled paper. He dropped them on the counter with a flourish. I could see names scribbled on them.

"I want to know how things turned out for all these patients," he said. "I want to know if they survived or not, whether I suggested the correct thing to do, if I was right about what was wrong with them. But there are *so many* of them."

For hours afterwards, during the drive back to Strawberry Plains, I couldn't get Jay's lament out of my head. His struggle was to be right about what was *wrong*.

26

I'd spent years obsessed with being right about what was *right*—as a law clerk for the U.S. District Court in Miami, an inner city prosecutor in Washington, DC, and finally as a U.S. Senate counsel. I'd given up my search for answers a lot quicker than Jay had.

**The night is far gone; the day is at hand.
So then let us cast off the works of darkness
and put on the armor of light.
Romans 13:12**

LAND OF THE GIANTS

Two years later

The Central Reading Room was awash in bones as usual. This time, when my eyes adjusted to the murk, the first thing I made out was a row of lightboxes covered with images of really big hands, giant hands, twice the size of mine.

The elongated skeletal fingers were terrifying. I acted calmer than I felt when I nodded toward them, asking, "Whose hands are those?"

"Patients with arthritis," Jay said. "We make enlargements for the rheumatologists. They prefer them, the better to see tiny erosions."

"Oh, thank goodness," I said, relieved. "I thought you'd discovered a mutant cousin of Bigfoot!"

I saw what might've been a hint of a smile, but I couldn't be sure.

After listening to Jay dictate for a while, I realized I was getting confused about an anatomical term he seemed to be using to describe two totally different things.

I asked him about it and it turned out he was saying two different words that sounded alike—coronal and carina. He tried to explain some of his most frequently used terminology, the jargon indicating the placement of a ventilator tube or orientation of the slices depicted in an x-ray or a scan.

Coronal indicated the slice was taken the plane of a pair of headphones. *Carina* referred to the place in the chest before the trachea divided into two branches that was critical in confirming whether or not a ventilator tube was placed properly.

"In the early days," Jay said, "we were only able to take through-and-through shots from the front, back, or side. Now we're 3D. We can take any number of tiny slices in axial, coronal, or sagittal sections.

"Sagittal slices are taken in the plane that an archer would hold a bow, horizontal axial orientations are taken in slices like salami, and coronal orientations are slices made like paper dolls or gingerbread men."

When I got tired of sitting I supplemented my anatomical training by consulting the skeleton hanging in the corner. It was a nice model, on the short side, but it looked pretty realistic. I touched it gingerly to see what it was made of.

It didn't seem to be actual bone, but I couldn't be sure so I examined it in the dim light. The rib cartilage seemed to be made of red plastic. Then I noticed *Made in Germany* stamped on one of the pelvic bones.

I decided to call the skeleton Hans.

I returned to a rolling chair beside Jay and listened to him blabber into a new style of recording device. I knew engineers had been working for more than forty years on voice recognition software intended specifically for radiologists because it had been the holy grail when I was in college studying for a degree in Biomedical Engineering. Only now was it becoming truly functional in the reading rooms.

As usual Jay spoke like he was on speed. I could barely understand him. I marveled that a computer could correctly interpret the spaces between sentences, words, and syllables. It could understand regional and national accents from around the world.

During the night I watched how the system worked. Jay would dictate and then punch some keys to review the computer-generated transcript of what he'd said.

Sometimes the system would erroneously transcribe a word or two. He would use a mixture of keyboard cursors and the handset to re-dictate the parts that were wrong, sometimes needing several tries to get the system to render them properly.

Every now and again he couldn't get the computer to recognize a word after several tries, so he'd have to type the correction into the system manually.

He dictated something about soft tissue that I didn't understand and when he was finished I asked him about it.

"We can see bone injuries on plain x-rays," he said, "but we can't necessarily see damage to veins and arteries, or nerves, or ascertain the magnitude of the soft tissue injury. The images of the bones might look okay, but the attending physician who's with the actual patient lying there on the gurney, may find a soft tissue injury that's not fixable, even something so serious they'll have to amputate a limb.

"In many cases the condition of the bone isn't the primary problem. A patient might have a horrible injury to a nerve, a destroyed brachial plexus, for example. You can see that on an MRI and understand that the person is never going to be able to use his arm again. But you can't see it on an x-ray.

"There can be a significant disproportion between the visible findings on an x-ray and the magnitude of the actual injury.

Jay glanced down at his pager, and said, "Neonatal ICU," and we took off at high speed. When we arrived, he sat down in a cramped reading room, facing a dark wall of x-rays and then paused before flipping the light switches on. "There's a film up here you're not going to want to see. Close your eyes."

He'd never said anything like that before, but I trusted his judgment, so I closed my eyes. I heard him flip the switches and then roll the conveyor to a new position. "It's okay now. You can open your eyes."

Jay was standing up, leaning in close to an x-ray of a newborn. He touched the film and his hand was the same size as the entire body of the baby. I was shocked. He touched the film gently, as if it was the child itself he was handling instead of a picture.

"They were concerned about a pneumothorax, but this little guy's fine." He picked up the phone, punched some numbers, and talked to a real person somewhere. Then he pointed to another film for my benefit as he made some additional comments about *double diapering*.

When he hung up, I asked, "What did they think was wrong with the baby?"

"Someone was worried that the child had a collapsed lung. The x-ray clearly showed two fully-inflated lungs. They could see that as well as I could, but an expert had to be called in immediately to confirm it."

"Why do they ask you to respond as if it was an emergency to something that's obvious?"

"Lawyers," he said smirking, getting even with me. And of course he was right. It was one of the reasons I'd stopped being a lawyer.

"And the diapering thing?"

"This little girl over here has a congenital hip dislocation, but if they put her in double diapers immediately, and keep her in them, it'll hold her legs in the proper position and the joint will fix itself.

"Kids are so plastic, she'll never have any problems with it the future. It'll be like it never happened."

I watched as Jay tarried over each of the x-rays. He clearly loved the babies.

"What didn't you want me to see?" I asked.

"Anencephaly."

The word sounded like a woman's name but I knew it must mean something terrible. "What is that?" I asked, wincing in advance.

"Some babies are born missing most of their brains."

"Why?"

"I don't know," he said softly. "It's a horrible thing, and fatal. There's gotta be meaning in it, but I'd be the last person to figure out what it is. The only mercy is that events around this particular child can't continue for more than a day or so."

I let that sink in. I'd been born cross-eyed and lived for many years seeing people flinch when I turned to face them. I was ashamed to be hiding from a baby, protecting myself from the sight of a human being who might not live for more than a day. Out of respect for the dying child and the shattered parents, I asked, "May I see?"

Jay stepped on the floor pedal and I watched dozens of films roll by until the rolling stopped. I looked for a few long moments and said a silent prayer for the tiny baby and his family.

Neither Jay nor I spoke. Then he flipped the lights off and we left.

I shadowed him for a couple more hours then decided to call it a night. I took a nap when I got home and woke up in the afternoon with a hangover. I felt guilty knowing he'd be at the hospital again in a few hours, while I could come and go as I pleased.

Therefore whatever you have said in the dark shall be heard
in the light,
and what you have whispered in private rooms
shall be proclaimed on the housetops.
Luke 12:3

THE BONE PHONE

Three years later

Everything was the color of moonlight. Unfortunately the illumination wasn't coming from the night sky. It was coming at Jay from the wall, striking him sideways. The monk was back on his knees again, inches from the crawling tank treads, utterly vulnerable to the relentless approach of a dreadnought that loomed constantly but never quite arrived, talking endlessly to the skeletons in a rapid monotone.

I looked at the ever-present wall of x-rays and tried to take in a portion of the deafening visual noise. Radiology had become a battle against a snowballing onslaught of pictorial information. Jay's efforts to keep up with it were like trying to sip water from a fire hose.

Nevertheless, and despite everything I'd learned about the cruel reality of the images, it was still not possible for me to see them as anything less than magnificent. They were so gloriously sharp, so beautifully human.

An hour later I finally got the courage to stand up and, for the first time, leaned in close to the pictures. At point-blank range I could see that each bone was a sack of powdered minerals tightly compressed by a clear, bone-shaped wrapper.

During the hours of Jay's shift I contemplated the soft glow characteristic of a reading room. It was a glamorous and distinctive shimmer.

Until recently the color was created quite literally by silver. It could be scraped off by x-ray recyclers and bars of silver metal would be left behind. My mother and father had an ingot of silver from a batch of x-rays they'd sent for recycling in the '80s.

The recyclers took thousands of traumas, years of human misery, and melted them all down into a single shiny nugget worth a lot of dough. I reminded myself that the pretty silver-plated portraits I was admiring were of patients who were elsewhere in the building straining to take another breath, or in terrible pain, wondering when it would stop.

The Central Reading Room was so large Jay had to move to a new telephone every couple of hours as he worked his way down the long counters. He'd read films and dictate his findings, slowly stretching a phone cord as he went. When he'd gone as far as the line would reach, he'd have to hang up one phone and dial in to the voice recognition system from another one.

I spaced out to the sounds of his dictation and the occasional muffled noises from the outside world—announcements over the hospital loudspeaker, telephones ringing, voices from down the hall. I tried to take all the sounds in at once like a vast radiological opera.

I'd be jarred back to the present whenever Jay stopped talking, especially if he went back to change the last few words of his dictation. He might make a correction because the transcription was faulty, or it might be because he'd thought of a better way to say what he was seeing.

He'd fall silent, punch buttons on the phone to rewind, then playback a portion of the recording. When it got to the words he wanted to change, he'd resume speaking. Each maneuver—stop, go, forward, backward—provoked a particular coded set of beeps I could hear coming through his handset.

"What's the name for that microphone thing," I asked, "the handset you're always holding?"

"We call it *The Bone Phone*," he said, smiling.

I had a growing sense of unease on account of the fact that none of Jay's patients ever moved. They all just hung there—still, silent, suspended forever in a single moment. None of them ever spoke, coughed, scratched, took a breath, or even had a heartbeat.

The reading room was a special sort of sensory deprivation tank.

In the becalmed environment, Jay's smallest movements were noticeable. He often sat perfectly still while reading the films. Scanning, scanning—with just his eyes moving. Occasionally he'd jiggle his left leg or he might stand up briefly to determine the size of something, either by estimating it against the known measurements of his own hand or by using a clear plastic metric ruler.

All the while, people who were barely more than wraiths took advantage of the darkness to slip into the room and quietly drop off stacks of films behind his back. I suspected he heard them, but he never appeared to notice that the pile of images was being renewed faster than he was able to deal with what he already had.

I continued to visit Hans, the plastic German skeleton, when I wanted to puzzle out something Jay had dictated. Hans was a creepy sort of unstuffed animal I played with to keep from falling asleep.

"This place is like a morgue," I blurted, when the night was far gone and the odd vibe of the big room overpowered my discretion. "It's too still and quiet. Nobody ever moves, not even Hans. How do you stand it?"

"Oh, they move," Jay said. "And when they do it blurs the films. We don't hang many of blurry ones, for obvious reasons, so you're not seeing them."

Then he turned around, and asked, "Who's Hans?"

"That's Hans," I said, pointing to the dangling plastic skeleton.

"Oh," he said, then swiveled back to face his work. But in that quirky way of his that was on my mental list of Radiological Anti-Social Skills, even though his back was to me, he continued to explain about blurred x-rays.

"The sicker the people are, the more rapidly they're breathing. Excessive chest movement makes it more difficult to get a clear image. It's also nearly impossible to avoid blurring when the patient's drunk or brain damaged."

"You x-ray drunks?" I said.

"Oh yeah. Lots of them. After they screw up the highways, they arrive here and foul up our lives as well. One night I had one literally tear up the CT scanner. He was a big strong guy and he was ripping pieces off the machine. I wanted to cancel the study right there, figuring if he was feeling that lively, he couldn't be hurt very bad, but the surgeon insisted on getting a scan.

"He had to send an anesthesiologist down to paralyze his patient so we could take a look. The surgeon was right, and I was wrong, four times over." Jay held up a hand and ticked off his mistakes on his fingers. "The guy had lacerated his liver, pancreas, spleen, and kidneys. He had an appalling list of internal injuries."

"How do you get a knockdown drug into a wild drunk?" I asked. "Do you give 'em a shot?"

"No," he said, shaking his head. "It's an I.V."

I raised my eyebrows, and he apparently saw the expression with eyes in the back of his head because he explained that, too.

"When we have to," he said, "we can muster enough personnel to isolate an arm and get the drugs into the patient. Drunks are a big problem at this hospital. There's a whole science to paralyzing and intubating them."

I pondered the fact that I was actually able to carry on a conversation with the back of Jay's head.

As if to punish me for complaining about how quiet things were, Jay's beeper went off, summoning him to ultrasound. I followed him as he threaded the maze of hallways. We turned a corner and encountered a trauma team propelling a badly injured person on a gurney toward us at high speed.

We moved back against the wall to let them pass, but before they reached us, they turned into a room that was only a few feet from where we were standing. It was a CT scanner suite.

I looked at Jay to ask if I could watch. He nodded.

A highly synchronized team whisked the bleeding man off the gurney. One of the radiology technicians managed to drape the scanner table with a large plastic sheet an instant before the man touched down atop it.

The trauma team was covered from head to toe in protective gear. They wore blue plastic gowns that covered them from neck to ankles, surgical gloves, and clear plastic splash guards to shield their faces. Some of them hadn't bothered to fasten their gowns all the way down the back so the blue material billowed and fluttered around them at the slightest movement.

A couple of them went into the adjacent CT control room where they could observe their patient through a large glass window and watch the results of the scan. As soon as the doctors got the information they were looking for they barked out a series of orders from behind their face shields.

A youngish man I took to be a surgery resident reached for the phone with a bloody glove and dialed. He said something about an operating room and hung up. The team swooped back into the scanner room, whisked their patient off the table and onto a gurney, and took off.

I loved the way the peaceful blue gowns floated and furled as the team moved. It made them look like angels in flight. I asked Jay about the new type of surgical gowns they were wearing.

"Cloth is permeable to fluids," Jay said. "Plastic isn't, so it makes a better barrier to blood and germs. And it's disposable, so it doesn't have to be laundered."

They were still in view, racing down the hall, when the phone rang in the CT control room. Jay and I watched the tech frown at the bloody handset.

"That's one of the busiest phones in our department," Jay said, shaking his head.

The tech grabbed a wipe and gingerly picked up the gruesome, blood smeared handset, holding it away from his face. When he hung up he got more wipes and cleaned the phone thoroughly. Then he went into the scanner room and gathered up the bloody sheet and put it and the wipes into a bio-disposal container.

When Jay and I left he was still wiping up bloody drips and splashes, and gathering up bits of debris shed by the patient and his attendants during their brief stint in the scanner room.

The trauma team had gone to a lot of trouble to keep the blood off themselves, but their counter-measures didn't extend to the radiology department.

We resumed our interrupted trip to the far less stimulating world of ultrasound where Jay dipped into a darkened room illuminated only by several monitors. There was nothing on any of the screens that I could identify.

Jay sat beside a technician and they discussed the first image. It was an incomprehensible blur, said to be a sonogram of a patient's hip joint. Jay talked to the tech about it in an authoritative tone.

Then they reviewed a second image filled with random-looking black and white static that Jay ruled to be a normal gall bladder. He diagnosed an aortic aneurysm from a third picture that looked like a snowstorm in Antarctica.

When we were well away from the room, I whispered, "Jay, those images are ridiculous. They're un-interpretable."

He looked at the floor and smiled patiently.

"There are limits to my faith in technology," I said, "and we've hit the wall."

As we walked, he tried to explain how ultrasound worked. He talked a great deal and used a lot of hand waving, but all I got from it was that the stupendously sharp images from an MRI that I so ardently admired, weren't what they seemed. They weren't actual pictures of anything. They were *models* created mathematically by a computer.

"They're *averaged data* in the form of a picture," he said. "They aren't images like a photograph or an x-ray. They're images emitted after stimulation."

There was more babbling about the technique that went way over my head leaving only a vague impression that the patient's body was magnetized and then photographed as it emitted some sort of prolonged electronic sigh.

The techno-yakking made an MRI sound like a magnetic version of the weird after-image thing a television set did for a few seconds after you turn it off. Or what happened to your eyes immediately after you closed a laptop in a dark room.

I regained consciousness as he was saying, "Sometimes, if an artifact is on the extreme left edge of the body, an MRI will depict it on the right.

"What? Like the carriage return on a type writer?"

"More like line-wrapping on a word processor. It happens when the patient is quite large. A hip will wrap. There might be anywhere from two to four superimposed images of a hip on the same side of the image."

"It gives you three butts on one side and none on the other?

"Yes."

"That's cruel," I said. "So, for heavy people, MRI's are contraindicated?"

"Not contraindicated. It's just that if a patient is especially large, a bit less information might be available due to the distortion in the hip region."

I shook my head. This was the radiological worst-case-scenario of *Does this outfit make me look fat?*

> We work in the dark—we do what we can—we give what we
> have.
> Our doubt is our passion, and our passion is our task.
> The rest is the madness of art.
> Henry James

DON'T TOUCH IT

Four years later

Jay couldn't type very well. He hated computers and wanted nothing to do with them. Unfortunately for him the entire radiology department was being converted into a digital wonderland.

There were good aspects to the conversion, too, of course. It would speed things up tremendously. All the widely dispersed reading rooms would be connected to a central location.

The clinical reason for the image would be available so he would know if the patient was *sick* or *injured*. That bit of information alone would be a cosmic breakthrough. He'd be clear about what the referring physician wanted him to look for. And he might get the patient's medical history.

The new system relied on high-resolution monitors that were mounted on end, so they were taller than they were wide. The reason radiologists rotated the monitors was obvious. It made more sense to encounter the images man-to-man rather than allowing the skeleton to recline.

Why force the doctor to read bilateral images sideways, when *left* and *right* were so important? If there was no rest for the radiologist, there would be no rest for the skeletons either.

When I arrived Jay was using his right index finger, the only finger he could type with, to press the same button over and over as fast as possible. I sat down behind him and then leaned around until I could see what he was pecking away at. It was a cursor.

When I looked up at the screen I saw he was taking a high-speed fantastic voyage through someone's body via a CT.

He'd cursor up for thirty or forty slices and then back down again. He repeated the round trip several times.

Then he picked up a telephone and called the ER and told the person on the other end of the line that it was a stone. For my benefit, he pointed at the tiny bright white speck on the screen that appeared in a single frame and disappeared when he cursored to the slices on either side of it.

Jay drew a digital box around the image and the computer told him how big the stone was. He said something to the ER about millimeters, which I couldn't convert to inches without exerting myself. It looked to me like the stone was no bigger than a speck of dust or a single bad pixel.

Watching the individual slices of the patient's body flash by reminded me of the elevator in the tallest department store in Knoxville. When I was a child and there was still a uniformed human attendant who operated the ornate brass cage, each time the elevator stopped and the door opened, the driver announced the type of goods sold on that floor. "Fourth Floor: Ladies' Foundations, China, and Silver."

Previously Jay had to create this same sort of anatomical mapping in his head. He'd look at the twenty frames printed on a single piece of flat film, and check how thick the slices were—three millimeters, seven millimeters. Then he'd mentally stack them and create a flipbook in his imagination.

I found his talent flabbergasting. Now the flipbook was computerized so I could see it, too, sort of.

The speed at which Jay punched through the slices made you feel like you were flying through someone's body from collarbone to thigh. It was a thrill ride in a tiny jet plane that was not just hugging the ground, trying to stay beneath the radar, but flying *below the surface*. These images displayed what was underneath the skin.

At first, I could interpret only one thing—the outline of the outer edge of the body. As you moved from the head toward the feet on the upper side of the body, the chest grew taller with each slice and then subsided. We crossed the relatively featureless plains of the stomach, got a quick glimpse of a depression at the belly button, and then a split appeared at the Great Rift Valley where the body divided into separate legs.

The outline of the back was much harder for me to orient myself on. I was unable to identify any of the internal organs from a thin slice. The only area I could recognize was the crack in the butt cheeks.

Where previously Jay might have had to scan the image for anything and everything, with no information as to why the picture had been taken, now he was able to know the primary symptom—sometimes.

Clearly the transition was still in progress because in between looking at the computer screen he loaded plain films onto the lightbox. If he happened to pull out an x-ray upside down, he'd toss the big floppy sheet into the air with one hand like a skilled pizza maker, spinning it 180 degrees.

Sometimes he'd stand up to study the films. He'd lean in close and absently flick the clear plastic retaining wires that held the pictures flat against the light, like plucking a banjo string.

During this visit I learned that a CT wasn't an actual picture either. It was a type of map created from averaged densities. The issue arose when I was startled by what the computer produced as a default image for data it didn't understand.

When it was confused, the scanner would depict a great blinding sunburst. A pacemaker, for example, didn't appear as a box of hardware. Instead it was displayed as a radiant sun inside a person's chest. I enjoyed the image, but suspected the cardiologists did not.

We were back in the Central Reading Room. Tonight it was heavily populated by the elderly—people with skin so deeply wrinkled that crevices and folds were visible on the x-rays. I allowed myself to think only compassionate thoughts about this because I knew I was looking my own future, if I should live so long.

Patients who were standing up were sagging and stooped. These people had lots of old injuries, like bone scars, alongside the new problems. Seeing the wasting bodies and demineralizing bones made my own mortality weigh heavily on me.

I stared at an x-ray of an old woman's spine. Her backbones were collapsing onto themselves in an extremely slow motion version of one of those high-rise buildings that was demolished a floor at a time with carefully synchronized dynamite blasts so the levels would pancake, one atop the other. Less mess that way. No injury to innocent bystanders.

I tried to imagine what the lady looked like on the outside and what her life was like. The enforced distancing from the patient was turning out to be nearly as painful as being there in person. That surprised me.

"This is all so strange," I said.

"Hmm?" Jay murmured, without turning around.

"I don't know. Something about the way you sit in a dark room by yourself examining people you'll never know or even meet. And you examine them from the inside out! It's wonderful that you can help them without having to cut them open or hurt them.

"But it's weird that you to have to do everything without seeing if the person is flushed or pale, or being able to feel if they're hot. The *not being there* gets to be a burden. You can't even ask them the simplest question!"

He nodded.

"What would you like to be able to ask them?" I asked.

"Where does it hurt?"

I burst out laughing. What an absurd handicap he had to work with. It was ridiculous.

"What else?"

"What kind of surgery have you had?"

"Can't you tell?"

"Sure. Sometimes you can, if it's something obvious. But it's usually not. They'll have a lot of staples at a place where there's no gallbladder or appendix and things will be rearranged. But often I'm trying to figure out why they hurt without knowing if they've had surgery for cancer, a bowel obstruction, or an ulcer. It makes me crazy."

I thought about the ridiculous inefficiency of his situation. Even with the highest tech in the hospital, the most basic facts were missing.

"The thing that gets to me the most," I said, "is that these people are all so beautiful—even when they're dying."

A reading room was a singular environment. Outwardly it was still but inwardly it was emotionally and psychologically moving. Aside from the morgue it was the quietest place in the hospital. It was like an art museum. Each body was a masterpiece—the shadows of the person's skin and muscles, the graceful curves of a shoulder blade, pelvis, or collarbone.

At first I was frightened by the pictures of skulls that appeared to be screaming, but then Jay told me the patients' mouths were held wide open so he could see their neck bones without their teeth blocking the view.

The intimacy of it was extremely affecting. It was a holy place.

"You never touch them," I mumbled. "Daddy said his patients couldn't get well if he didn't touch them. He said he learned over the years that he had to touch the place they were talking about, or they wouldn't get well."

Jay nodded. I knew he gave the other doctors good information. I hoped they would touch the patient for him. I wanted to reach out and touch him, for whatever good it could do, but I didn't.

This was the land where blood could be black, like the blood in the *Odyssey*, but in this place there was even black pee and black barf and black whatever else you could think of.

And yet nothing ever got on you. That was my father's world, the world I'd grown up in, the world of *on ya*. Body fluids got all over you in a family doctor's office. This place made me miss that.

I wasn't the only one who felt that way, either. When I told my father some of the things I'd seen in the radiology department and how it felt, he told me about one of his family doctor pals who'd moved away to train as an orthopedist.

A few years later, they guy had come back home and resumed the practice of family medicine. My father was startled to see him again and asked him what had happened. "I missed getting stuff on me," he said.

I shared this vignette with Jay.

"You want some on ya?" he asked. "You have no idea. I can't even show you the worst of it because it wouldn't be appropriate, but if you only knew. We call them *code browns*, barium enemas gone awry. But, if you like, I can show you a little bit of the hands-on work I do."

I was vastly relieved to learn that there were some types of imaging where a patient and a radiologist were actually in the same room.

"You'll have to hang around until the day shift starts," Jay said, "but I'll show you some fluoroscopy."

Part of Jay's job was to teach fluoroscopy to residents. He let me go with him to one of the fluoroscopy suites. Just inside the anteroom was a steel rack that held an array of gear—lead vests, kilts, aprons, and thyroid shields

Jay and a young resident suited up in the heavy protective clothing and went into the adjacent room where the scope was. I stayed in the anteroom to watch the proceedings through a large glass window.

Jay helped the resident make several x-ray movies, each of which was only a few seconds long. They were trying to determine why a teenager was having trouble swallowing.

I'd never seen anyone perform fluoroscopy before, but the difference between Jay's skill level and the resident's was painfully obvious. Jay was fast and smooth at manipulating the huge camera and at perfectly timing short bursts of radiation to capture the crucial seconds during the patient's attempt to swallow.

The resident was awkward, both at moving the machine and at knowing when to take the pictures. Afterwards I mentioned it, and Jay said, "He's just starting out. He'll get better."

I had to smile. It was a classic medical moment. The experienced older guy working alongside a younger fellow to transfer the skills of healing.

I followed Jay back to the Central Reading Room so he could finish some minor clerical tasks before calling it a day. In a quiet moment I asked, "What's the worst x-ray you've ever seen?"

He lowered his handset and thought about it. "Motorcycle accidents where fingers and legs are amputated by the impact. Or men in their seventies and eighties who turn farm tractors over on themselves."

I winced at that. My father still worked on our farm with a tractor and he was in his eighties.

"They work too far into the evening. And they're too old to be able to jump clear of the machinery when something goes wrong.

"I remember one old guy who fell off his tractor while it was moving. The back wheels ran over him, giving him serious crush injuries. And the engine stayed on, so even though the tractor no longer had a driver, it continued to move around the field.

"Here's the truly nightmarish part. Somehow it rolled in a big circle. The guy was so severely injured, he couldn't get out of the way, so it ran over him again!

"Most of his ribs were broken and he had terrible internal injuries but somehow he survived. A few weeks later he was able to walk out of the hospital."

Jay's voice trailed off and I waited, watching his eyes flicker as he searched his vast mental gallery for more terrible images.

"I looked at an x-ray of my father's chest," he said, slowly. "It was the first time I'd ever read an image of someone in my own family. I saw that he had multiple lesions. Cancer.

"I shouldn't have been, but I was shocked at how much difference it made to know the patient. To know what an image like that meant for the person and their family."

He fell quiet for several seconds, then said, "I care about all my patients. I try to give all of these images my utmost attention."

He waved at the images on display in front of him. "I take pride in being diligent and treating each image as if it were my own. But still, it was odd how different the experience felt when it was my own father facing me on the lightbox."

He stopped talking again, obviously lost in thought. I waited for him to resume dictating, but he didn't. Finally, he said, "Then a few years later I had the occasion to see an image with a terrifying anomaly and . . . it was me."

46

I couldn't prevent myself from recoiling slightly in surprise.

He turned ninety degrees, showing me the side of his face, and said, "We all have defects that we may or may not have the occasion to discover—things that might cause trouble or even physical death—problems that even if you can find them, the extent of the damage they will cause is unknown or unknowable.

"I have a . . ."

Suddenly the remarkable precision of his vocabulary vanished, as well as his formidable descriptive powers. He seemed unable to speak.

After a long pause, he swallowed, and said, "I have an . . . abnormality.

"It's beginning to give me symptoms," He touched his chest, and added, "I had a tech help me do a scan one night.

"When I saw the image, at first I couldn't take it in. It was like the whole world just stopped."

He put the handset down on the counter in front of him. "It was hard to feel anything or even think. I just stared at the picture, hearing this voice in inside my head saying, *That's me! That's me.*"

I asked in a whisper, "Can they fix it?"

He shook his head.

"I took the images to a specialist at Mass General for a consult." He made a wry smile, and added, "They're still in the trunk of my car. I don't want to file them here for other people to see."

"What did the specialist say?"

"*Wow.*"

I felt faint.

Jay looked composed, but there was no color in his face. His skin appeared translucent and his gray eyes were silver. He stared with no expression. He had a good poker face, but I knew what that meant.

I screwed my own poker face on tight and asked, "What else did he say?"

"He said it was the biggest *one of those* he'd ever seen and that I needed to be careful." Jay was blinking rapidly and the muscles in the side of his jaw were clenching and releasing.

"He said, 'Don't touch it. Don't let anybody touch it.' That means no operations or radiation treatments.

Oh, God, I thought, *this was the source of his bias toward* -omas. *Jay had an* -oma.

"It's in a difficult location. They can't get to it."

Then he swiveled back toward the monitor, picked up the handset, and resumed his dictation. I sat behind him for a long time, silent, until he finished dictating. When he stood up to leave, I said, "Can I see the images?"

He nodded. We went outside. It was morning and the sun was shining. It was painfully bright after we'd been in the dark for so long.

It was the first time I'd ever seen Jay in daylight. The difference was startling. I wasn't sure I would've recognized him if we hadn't walked outside together.

He seemed more human now that I could see the red blood vessels in his eyes and the flush on his cheeks. And he seemed more vulnerable out here where there were colors and other people and everything was moving.

We took an elevator to the top of a huge parking garage and then walked to the far corner of the lot. This level was open to the sky and had a superb view of the hospital complex and downtown. Jay retrieved a large brown envelope from the trunk of a white Porsche. It was stamped *Hospital Radiology Department. Do Not Remove.* He stood facing me, holding it.

When he didn't offer it to me, I said, "Let me see," and gently pulled the big envelope out of his hands. Then I reached inside and removed one of the pieces of film.

"We can't look at these out here!" he said.

"Sure we can," I said, and held the MRI up to the sky.

"I've never read a film using the sun before," he laughed. "You won't be able to see anything."

"Sure I will," I said.

I scanned the twenty images in a vague, helter-skelter fashion, looking for something, anything that would jump out at me. But of course nothing did. "Show me," I said.

He indicated two of the frames.

"What am I looking at?" I asked.

"See this?" he said pointing toward the middle of one of the images.

I saw a greyish blob, surrounded by some other blobs, but I had no idea what I was seeing.

"Are you scared?" I asked.

"Yes."

I still had trouble correlating images with the location on a real person, so as I slipped the film back into the envelope, I asked, "Where is it exactly?"

He gestured with his index fingers, one in front pointed toward his heart and the other under his left arm pointed into his chest, saying, "It's at the intersection of these two lines."

When he dropped his hands I reached out and gently touched his white coat over the place he'd indicated.

Later, when I pulled out of the parking lot, the little booth at the exit was empty, and the slender barrier was sticking straight up in the air, saluting me as I left the premises. I returned the salute and drove away.

I was lucky to make it home alive. I couldn't decide where to focus my attention. I kept making steering mistakes because I was seeing everything as one great whole with no particular part more important than any other.

I caught myself slowing down in the fast lane and once I sat waiting at a green light until someone came up behind me and blew their horn.

I tried to imagine how a radiologist would cope with the downstream effects of seeing a radiograph of his own body that left him powerless in the face of deeply disturbing information.

Would he have better tools to handle the situation?

Would ignorance have been bliss?

I made the last leg of the long drive in a dense fog. During certain times of the year East Tennessee was blanketed with low-lying clouds from dawn to mid-morning.

As I drove through the swirling mist I thought about the extraordinary power a two-dimensional black and white image had. It could fundamentally alter one's perception of the future.

A person could collapse under the weight of an acute consciousness of their own mortality or use the new awareness to grow as a human being. I hoped I'd be able to meet scary situations with as much grace and courage as Jay. And I prayed for him every night for years.

**I would rather walk with a friend in the dark,
than alone in the light.
Helen Keller**

MARS

Five years later

After another long gap between our meetings, Jay called me one evening out of the blue. He said he was trying to deal with his files. It was a big job, he said, and he could use some help.

He asked if I could come to the hospital.

Now? I wanted to ask, but didn't. Instead, I said, "I'll be there in three and a half hours."

He thanked me and hung up. I had no idea what the situation was, but I left immediately. It was just after midnight when I met him in the reception area just outside his office. There were a couple of wheeled stainless steel baskets that looked like a hospital version of grocery carts.

He led me into his office and gestured toward the shelves packed with brown radiograph sleeves that covered two entire walls from floor to ceiling. He explained that these were his teaching files—more than thirty years of images carefully curated for their value as educational examples for the residents.

He was retiring and had been asked to destroy his files before he left. The hospital was now totally digital and his collection of films were perceived as useless relics from another age.

From the few telegraphic comments he made I gleaned that he was in an distressing bind—although his files were seen by his successors as so much garbage taking up space, their destruction had to be done a careful, ritualistic way because they contained private patient information.

He didn't say it straight out, but it was obvious he didn't want to do it. The mere thought of it was upsetting him. And for some reason he'd decided to ask me to help him do the dirty work.

I was touched and honored. Our friendship, such as it was, had now spanned fifteen years.

This sort of thing had happened several times before with doctors I'd interviewed for other books. After an interval of years with no contact, I'd get a call when they were in distress of some kind. Even if we'd talked for only an hour or two, there was something about the way I'd listened to them that created a bond.

I could understand it. Most people were never really listened to in their whole lives, not even for five minutes, and certainly not for prolonged periods of time without judgment. When you did that for someone, it was a holy thing, an event of eternal significance.

"Where do we start?" I asked.

His hands fluttered in a hopeless, helpless gesture, then he visibly steeled himself and stepped over to one wall and reached into the middle of a row at stomach level. He grabbed a handful of folders and jerked them out.

He tossed them onto a nearby table and picked up the topmost sleeve. He showed me what to do—remove the films and put them in one of the carts. Put the non-film items—the folder, notes, and any papers—in the other cart.

Then he stopped and waited for me to do the same. I reached for a handful of folders and tugged. Nothing happened. I tried harder and, again, nothing happened. I couldn't begin to shift the films with one hand. I tried half as many and was able to slide a few of the heavy, floppy folders out of the shelf.

Jay watched as I made a little stack of them on a table next to his and separated the contents like he'd showed me. I pulled out a film and set it into a cart.

His eyes flicked toward the image. Then he watched me set the folder aside. It was obvious something about what I did bothered him.

"Did I do it right?" I asked.

He nodded.

"What's wrong?" I asked.

I saw the muscles work in his jaw. He shook his head, then he went into professor mode as he explained that once a image was separated from the annotations on the folder and the papers inside, its value was lost. The *lesson* no longer existed.

It was an odd situation, and painful. Here we were, together again for a few hours in the radiology department in the middle of the night, but this time, instead of teaching me, he wanted me to help him dismantle the painstaking work of his professional life.

Together we would systematically destroy the physical repository of his hard-won wisdom. And there was a lot of it. I wanted to cry, but I didn't let myself for fear of making things worse for Jay.

As we worked he explained that he'd called me because I was a comedy writer and a doctor's kid. He thought I'd understand what was happening and how he felt about it, and yet still be able to crack jokes. He said he'd put the task off as long as he possibly could, the realized he'd never be able to get it done without some comic relief.

I pulled out a particularly beautiful piece of film that bore multiple images of an entire skeleton. I wondered how they'd shrunken the images to fit onto a single piece of plastic. And why?

One of the perfect little skeletons was just four or five inches tall. It was charming and spooky at the same time. "What's this?" I asked.

Jay glanced at it. "A nuclear bone scan of a young boy."

The muscles in his jaw clenched again. I decided not to ask him any more questions for the rest of the night. I just helped him shift hundreds of pounds of x-rays from the wall, to the carts, and then to the shredder. It was hard labor and tedious.

I tried to do the task mindlessly—just another gravedigger on the graveyard shift.

When we were done, he said, "Let's get out of here."

As usual I trailed along behind, rather than beside him. I always had trouble keeping up, and I guess I was letting him clear the path for me, as if we were making our way through dangerous terrain. Maybe we were.

I had no idea where Jay was heading, but then he turned and shoved a door open, and suddenly we were outside the hospital, standing on a concrete stoop in the dark. Apparently he was through for the night—maybe through forever.

He kept going. Gradually I realized he was headed for the parking garage. We rode an elevator to the top floor and then walked to the far corner where his car was parked all by itself.

He shrugged his white coat off and wadded it into a ball. He stood for a few moments holding it, staring out over the railing as if considering whether to hurl the coat off the roof of the ten-story garage, but then he opened his trunk and tossed it inside.

He looked up at the night sky, and said, "See that red thing? That's Mars."

I looked too low at first and saw a brilliant cherry red light. That couldn't be Mars, could it? It disappeared for a moment, then came back on, and I realized it was a blinking light atop a cell phone tower.

I tilted my head back and saw a more indistinct orange light that I suspected might be Mars. I was stunned that, to a radiologist, or at least to Jay, the entire world outside the hospital was just an extra-large reading room and the night sky was simply God's mighty x-ray.

I shook my head.

"That *is* Mars, I assure you."

"I believe you," I said. "I was just marveling that the heavens are yet another image you feel compelled to review. One last picture to read out before dawn."

Jay tried to smile, but I could tell he was miffed. He didn't need to be reminded that he had trouble winding down.

I took a deep breath and decided to give the guy a break. Who wouldn't need to reorient themselves when escaping from the underworld?

From where we stood we could see the bowl of the sky, as well as the lights of the vast hospital, and a dull glow from downtown. The windsock on the helipad snapped and fluttered sideways in the stiff breeze.

"It's cold," I said, shivering.

Jay rummaged around in the still-open trunk of his car and produced an old handmade quilt. He slammed the trunk closed, moved to stand close to me, and wrapped it around both of us.

"You know when you retire," I said, "you can give up this vampire lifestyle. You'll be free to go about in broad daylight, and sleep at night."

He frowned and nodded almost imperceptibly. Apparently the idea didn't have much appeal.

"And you can see people who are three-dimensional, in color, with their skins still on. I think you'll find that women look even better that way. Or most of them do."

He nodded again.

"The downside is that other people will be in the restaurants and you'll have to pay for your food."

He snorted.

"And no more retinue of silent attendants."

"Now *that* will be hard," he murmured.

"Will you miss the bones?" I asked.

"I don't know."

Now he was shivering.

By unspoken agreement we decided to sit down on the pavement next to his low-slung car and use it to block the wind. Jay readjusted the quilt around us and then pointed up into the sky and called out the names of several stars.

While we looked at them silenced ambulances came and went with their red strobes flashing and a helicopter landed and offloaded another poor soul.

I watched a few silver-rimmed black clouds race across the darkened sky and pondered the future of a reclusive monk facing retirement. How did one retire from being retired from the world?

Where did a hermit go when he wanted to retreat?

"What are you gonna do next?" I asked.

There was a long gap of silence, then Jay said, "I have no idea."

"What do you wanna do?"

He rested his head back against the car door and thought about it. "First, I'd like to sleep. I haven't had a decent night's sleep in years."

The wind ruffled the ends of his hair and he tugged the quilt up higher. "Then after I wake up I'm going to enjoy being resolutely and unashamedly *bad* at something that doesn't matter."

"An endeavor where no lives are hanging in the balance?" I said.

"Exactly. And I want to be able to take my time," he said. "I want to be able to wander around aimlessly and loiter and *not* have to stare at sickness and death all day—not mine and not anyone else's."

I could certainly understand where he was coming from. "You could take exotic vacations," I suggested.

"That's such a stereotype. And anyway I wouldn't know where to begin."

"You could start with familiar environments like ossuaries and catacombs, and gradually work your way above ground."

He snorted.

"You could rent a cabin inside the Arctic Circle and spend the winter gradually adjusting to daylight."

He smiled at that.

"You could go to the beach and get used to seeing three-dimensional women in color with their skin on. And then maybe someday take a trip to a mall so you could stare at bodies that were fully clothed.

He grunted.

"You could wear your doctor coat and go to Comic-Con and *pretend* to pretend to be a doctor. You could stand in line to buy the newest iProduct. You could go to cheerleading camp."

Jay laughed out loud. It was a rusty sound.

I stopped talking, but we continued to sit there in the cold, dark, windy space, sharing the quilt, until I felt his weight shift slightly against my shoulder. I glanced over and noticed he'd nodded off to sleep.

His face was peaceful and his breathing was deep and even. It was a nice moment and a good start. Jay's retirement had begun just as he'd hoped, with some long needed rest.

***

This small narrative is a companion to a larger work entitled *Radiologists at Work: Saving Lives with the Lights Off*—a collection of memorable moments from twenty radiologists in more than half a dozen subspecialties covering a period of over seventy years of practice, from the 1940s to the present day.

About the Author

4-Time Wall Street Journal best selling author of heartwarming and heartbreaking memoir, biography, and mystery. Carolyn Jourdan chronicles miracles, mayhem, comedy, tragedy, and madcap medical moments in Appalachian medicine, as well as zany and touching interactions with wildlife in the Great Smoky Mountains National Park.

Jourdan's trademark blend of wit and wisdom, humor and humanity have earned her high praise from Dolly Parton and Fanny Flagg, as well as major national newspapers, the New York Public Library, Elle, Family Circle Magazine, and put her work at the top of hundreds of lists of best books of the year and funniest books ever.

Carolyn is a former U.S. Senate Counsel to the Committee on Environment and Public Works and the Committee on Governmental Affairs. She has degrees from the University of Tennessee in Biomedical Engineering and Law. She lives on the family farm in Strawberry Plains, Tennessee, with many stray animals.

Carolyn's first book: "Heart in the Right Place" is a #7 Wall Street Journal best seller and #1 in Biography, Memoir, Science, Medicine, and Doctor-Patient Relations on Amazon.

The follow-up, "Medicine Men: Extreme Appalachian Doctoring," is a #5 and #6 Wall Street Journal best seller and #1 in Biography, Memoir, Science, Medicine, and Doctor-Patient Relations on Amazon, as well as an Amazon All-Star.

"Bear in the Back Seat: Adventures of a Wildlife Ranger in the Great Smoky Mountains National Park" is a #9 Wall Street Journal best seller and #1 in Science, Biology, Animals, Bears, and Travel Biography on Amazon.

"Bear Bloopers: True Stories from the Great Smoky Mountains National Park" is Jourdan's most recent book of true escapades of black bears and rangers in the Great Smoky Mountains National Park.

"Out on a Limb: A Smoky Mountain Mystery," is a #6 in the USA best seller and #1 in Mystery, Cozy Mystery, and Medical Fiction on Amazon.

Visit her at www.CarolynJourdan.com and hear her read stories from her books.

http://facebook.com/CarolynJourdan
http://facebook.com/CarolynJourdanAuthor
http://twitter.com/CarolynJourdan

Made in the USA
Middletown, DE
21 December 2016